DON'T MANAGE ME, #UNDERSTANDME

Leveraging the Gen Y mindset and making it work within your organization

@JASONSMORGA AND @LANCEJRICHARDS

CONTENTS

PAGE 6 | Introduction

PAGE 8 | Gen Y foundation: Continuous feedback and reinforcement

PAGE 14 | Gen Y heart: It's all about connection

PAGE 18 | Gen Y reach: The access-all-areas mindset

PAGE 22 | Gen Y footsteps: What moves and motivates them?

PAGE 28 | Gen Y head: What are they thinking?

PAGE 32 | The workplace collision

PAGE 34 | Conclusion

YOU'VE READ PLENTY ABOUT GEN Y ALREADY. YOU GET IT. THE GENERATIONS ARE WIRED DIFFERENTLY, THEY WORK DIFFERENTLY AND ORGANIZATIONS HAVE TO ADAPT. **GOT IT.**

So, you've been working on your adaptation strategies…how's that working out so far? Have you started to see progress within your organization? How about within your department? We know the typical response—it's out of your direct control, right? What about those factors that are within your control? Have you personally made any changes in the way you manage or interact with Gen Ys?

The simple fact is, you don't have much time to change. Improving productivity, reducing turnover and building your talent supply chain across younger age groups is imperative for organizational success as we move into the next decade.

When preparing this paper, we were mindful of just how much has already been published about generational issues in the workplace. That's why we reviewed more than 30 existing papers, studies and surveys—from leading think tanks to Big Four consulting firms—to find out if there really is a consensus on how to manage Gen Y (and beyond).

We consumed a seemingly limitless supply of articles in various periodicals, ranging from *The Economist* to a one-paragraph blurb from patch.com. We also (shockingly) spoke with real, live Millennials—from entry-level employees at a San Francisco-based energy company, to MBA students in Bangkok and undergraduates in Detroit. And, we made good use of the *Kelly Global Workforce Index*, an annual primary research exercise for Kelly, which, in 2012 included approximately 45,000 Gen Y respondents from more than 30 countries. We even had real, live Millennials read drafts of this paper—amazingly we passed.

From all of this research, we can tell you that there are fundamental reasons why organizations, not just HR departments and leaders, must respond to generational issues. We can also tell you why some of the strategies that were supposed to work for Gen Y haven't. Take a deep breath, and prepare to stop 'managing' Gen Y employees, and start 'understanding' them.

LANCE JENSEN RICHARDS, GPHR, SPHR

JASON S. MORGA, PHR

GEN Y FOUNDATION: CONTINUOUS FEEDBACK AND REINFORCEMENT

Before we start talking about Gen Ys as if they are from another planet (although sometimes, after reading research, we may wonder), you need to understand how they grew up and how this has impacted their approach to working.

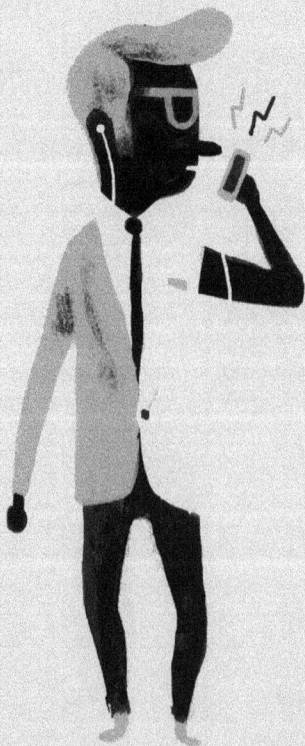

One key difference between growing up in the mid-1980s through to the 1990s and the 2000s (as opposed to previous decades), has been the way in which children have experienced self-directed play, and more importantly, risk and freedom.

Many studies and articles have discussed the increased emphasis during recent decades on the following elements of parenting and education:

Risk aversion

Positive feedback

Adult or parental supervision during play, then during school, and now at work (i.e. helicopter parenting)

Fundamentally, these parenting and educational trends have changed the way people now behave in the workplace—and this isn't Gen Y's doing. In fact, many of the complaints about how Gen Y now operates in the workplace come from the very individuals who pioneered these parenting and educational changes. Ironic.

However, we need to stop for a moment here and recognize that there is a big difference between parenting someone and being his or her boss. Simply raising a Gen Y individual does not prepare you for managing one in the workplace. Parenting and managing *are* different.

Instead, older generations must recognize that some of the foundations of their management style, and the messages they have heard from their HR department, are in fact reinforcing (rather than bridging), the generational divide.

Older workers have been trained to focus on issues of fairness and uniformity in their management style. In many ways, they've been asked to provide a homogenous experience of being managed; one where everyone is treated the same way. Yet, this is a recipe for failure in the Millennial workplace.

Instead, older managers need to develop a more individual approach, one that addresses the needs and motivations of individuals, not 'employees', as if they were one homogenous group with the same thoughts and motivations. After all, one Gen Y employee won't be the same as the next, and the real answer lies in finding appropriate ways to treat people fairly, but differently.

"

Yes, we Gen Ys need constant feedback, that's part of who we are, and it's part of what we're used to when we post things on social media. Tools like Facebook are just so powerful. Through them, I'm exposed to the details of hundreds of people's lives every second of the day. I'm constantly seeing how they're progressing and it makes me reflect on my own life and ask myself, 'How can I be better?'"

FREELANCE DIRECTOR, AUSTRALIA

In understanding the foundations of Gen Y, we cannot ignore the role of technology. While technology has influenced all of us, Gen Y has evolved with technology as a life center. It has particularly influenced their communication styles—partly because parents have been less inclined to let their children roam the outside world, and instead have allowed them to do so online, in the comfort and protection of their home.

Believe it or not, this hasn't always had disastrous outcomes. Millennials have developed a new version of community, friendship and connectivity. And, the networks they've learned to form are not always superficial, meaningless and disposable—the Arab Spring has proven this.

In October, 2010, we may have argued that these social networks are very broad and very popular, but that they were tenuous in nature. After the Arab Spring, it became clear that they aren't tenuous at all—they are tenacious. And they are powerful.

Gen Y's ability to build, shape, dismantle, evolve and grow networks quickly and easily is one thing. But their ability to create networks that are genuine forces for change is something else entirely. We often minimize social media as pure entertainment. It's not, and proficiency in using it is a skill that has genuine applications in the workplace—one that older generations have yet to fully grasp.

The foundations of Gen Y are different from the previous generations. They've been parented and educated differently, and the technology that may have influenced all of us has fundamentally shaped them. Broadly speaking, Gen Ys tend to value and expect:

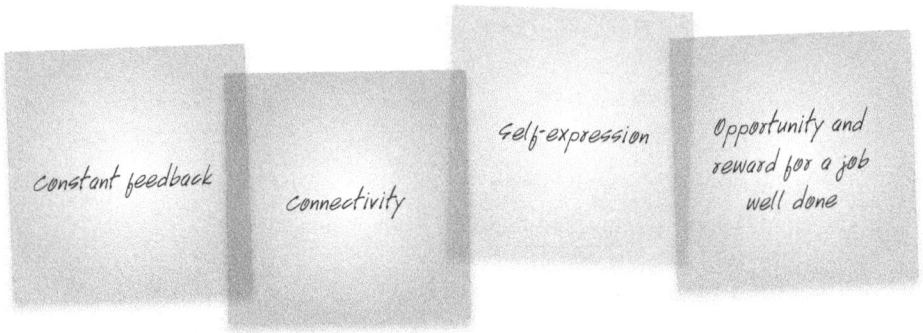

Constant feedback

Connectivity

Self-expression

Opportunity and reward for a job well done

This means that managers and organizations as entities have a new challenge. Instead of 'managing' Gen Ys, they need to deeply study what makes them tick on an individual level. They need to understand them, and this is something no generation ever does easily. However, if you understand the demographics, this time it's non-negotiable.

CORPORATE BRAND/REPUTATION IS KEY TO EVALUATING A POTENTIAL EMPLOYER (% YES)

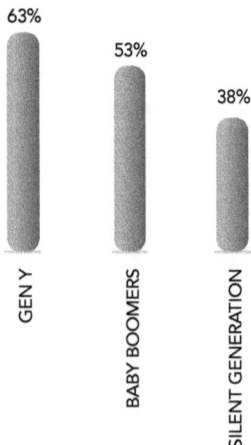

63%
53%
38%

GEN Y

BABY BOOMERS

SILENT GENERATION

HOW EMPLOYERS CAN RESPOND

Look at your own foundation: Corporate culture is the key consideration for all employees (regardless of age) when deciding whom to work for. Gen Y specifically looks for organizations that demonstrate strong market leadership and a corporate brand/reputation that resonates with them. So, it's important to critically analyze the way your brand is perceived in the market by all generations—especially by this young cohort. Have you crafted messaging that resonates with them? Or is your employer brand a one-size-fits-all entity? Of the Gen Y members surveyed, 63% said that corporate brand/reputation is a key way that they evaluate potential employers; just 53% of Baby Boomers and 38% of the Silent Generation say they do the same.

Think about different, ongoing forms of performance feedback: Performance discussions and review processes are notoriously difficult to get right. One-size-fits-all approaches are losing favor, and while the process must be fair, it must also be flexible enough to allow the individual to be understood, provided with the right feedback, and enabled to excel. Gen Y favors immediate and ongoing input in a smaller/shorter and more casual format so they know how they're progressing day-to-day and minute-to-minute, not year-to-year. Performance management is an ongoing process, not an event.

GEN Y HEART: IT'S ALL ABOUT CONNECTION

Gen Y places a high value on connections. In fact, a recent Cisco report found that roughly half of students and young professionals surveyed considered access to the internet nearly as important as water, food, air and shelter; and more than half of students felt that they could not live without the internet.

This is really tough for older generations to understand, but from their earliest childhood, members of Gen Y have used technology and devices to connect them with learning, knowledge, information, entertainment— and people.

Think for a moment about how you define a friend. For older generations, this is going to be significantly different, because technology has facilitated a different kind of experience of connection and friendship. For younger generations, keeping up-to-date with Facebook feeds is a way to connect; it is (again according to the Cisco report), a close second to actually spending time with people. Previous generations just didn't have the luxury of connecting with people in these ways—at least not as their ideas of how the world works were forming, and that's why they still don't totally get it.

It was well-educated and tech-literate Gen Xers and young Boomers that infused computing technology into the innovative learning environments of the young, blossoming Gen Ys. As the early 1990s passed, connection was no longer defined within the classroom or Local Area Networks (LAN) of Gen Ys inner circle. Instead, they were empowered to connect their imagination and learning environment with a global resource—the World Wide Web. This enabled Ys to interact with peers around the world on classroom projects, research studies and even extracurricular interests. And, just as many Ys were entering their high school years—when they were laying the foundations of their peer-to-peer relationships—the internet quite quickly transformed into an environment of 'user-generated content' and individual expression.

Today, connectivity is what Ys expect. They are the 'Now' generation because they can be. Instant gratification. Rising expectations for customization. Now. Now. Now. These are the expectations that Gen Y has become accustomed to. From pre-packaged foods to instant feedback on their social media posts, this generation is accustomed to a level of 'now' that previous generations just couldn't have—and it has made Gen Y more open, less concerned with privacy and less likely to keep their opinions to themselves.

As a digitally connected generation, Gen Y has also been afforded the luxury of exploring diversity for much of their formative years. This understanding and appreciation of cultural difference and inclusion has exposed them to social issues and diverse needs. Humanitarian causes, local/community-focused needs and social awareness have been, and continue to be, defining traits of the younger generation. The depth and reach of connectivity they have been able to achieve has helped them create meaning in their lives—shared meaning and commonality in even the most unlikely places.

The Gen Y heart is worn on its sleeve. It's there for all to see (and hopefully to 'like').

IN THEIR WORDS

Everyone wants to give back and feel like they are doing something good. Your job should involve helping people in some way, whether directly through the work, or through outside activities. This helps give you meaning."

MARKETING SPECIALIST, MIDWEST USA

HOW EMPLOYERS CAN RESPOND

Promote connectivity: Gen Y doesn't just approve of social media use at work, they often see it as work. It is the new form of relationship building and networking, and companies must learn to use it to their advantage. Find ways to use social media principles and tools for work purposes to fulfill the Gen Y need for consistent, ongoing input and dialogue with co-workers—regardless of rank or location. Crowd-sourcing answers to questions can now yield faster results than Googling a topic—and this is a skill that companies should exploit. Allowing younger workers to use these techniques to increase productivity is part of the solution, not the problem.

Use social media tools built for the workplace: There are many ways to harness the power of social media for the workplace. At Kelly Services, we've used 'Salesforce Chatter', which has proved successful and allowed people to connect across geographic boundaries, as well as across organizational silos.

GEN Y REACH: THE ACCESS-ALL-AREAS MINDSET

Hierarchies are great frameworks for organizing ourselves, but Gen Y's are less inclined to get them, or take them at face value. This is something corporate leaders really struggle to understand and it's no wonder—after all, what's the alternative?

For as long as anyone can recall, managers and leaders have been there to check, balance and guide decision making. They have more experience, deeper knowledge and can effectively weigh up a greater number of issues and choices. Right?

Well, we all know that managers differ vastly in their ability, motivations and style. This is the great weakness of hierarchical structures, and Gen Ys are much, much less tolerant of this structural issue within organizations. Instead, they prefer intricately connected, cross-functional ways of operating regardless of location, rank or role. They prefer dialogue and informality, and it's not because they're lazy or disengaged.

Instead, it's because they've had much more experience than the rest of us with making productive connections across traditional boundaries, as well as participating in global discussions about wide-ranging interests. They're generally more participative, and believe this is what organizations want and need from them.

"

IN THEIR WORDS

Some organizations have very rigid rules about whom you can speak to if you have an idea or want to fix a problem. It's frustrating when I have an idea but can't go directly to the person it's most relevant to. As I see it, it's a waste of time for the organization if my direct manager has to get involved to progress a solution. It devalues ideas; they should be taken on merit, not based on who has them."

COMMUNICATIONS ADVISOR, AUSTRALIA

They're not thinking, "It's all about me", they're thinking, "I need to contribute." And this is a critical difference. Baby Boomers might hear a self-centeredness in many of the ways that members of Gen Y speak and interact, but it's inherently about Gen Ys assumption that to be useful they must put up their hands and be heard.

The Gen Y reach is global, 24-7 and it's ready to join any conversation that seems relevant or interesting.

HOW EMPLOYERS CAN RESPOND

Be transparent about opportunities and change: There have been many articles written about Gen Y's FOMO tendencies—their 'Fear Of Missing Out'—and how this decreases loyalty and attentiveness to current tasks/ jobs. The constant connection that Gen Ys have to other conversations, knowledge, opportunities and networks makes it possible to always know what else is going on 'out there'. And, this increases Gen Y's anxiety about, and focus on, being involved in the best possible experience available to them. Whatever other generations might think about the FOMO mentality, it's critical to recognize the risk it poses to organizations that do not openly and effectively communicate opportunities that are available, as well as significant changes that are on the organizational agenda. Trying to reduce the FOMO effect is partly about communicating openly regarding the direction of the organization so that younger workers know that their job and their company is constantly evolving too.

GEN Y FOOTSTEPS: WHAT MOVES AND MOTIVATES THEM?

In recent PwC research, Millennials talked about 'compromise' in accepting jobs during the recent recession. Then they happily explained that they were looking for alternative employment. Our own research reflects this same trend—at least 50% of Millennials say they are 'always looking' for alternative employment, even when they are 'happy' with their current role.

So, if they're looking even when they're satisfied, what exactly are they looking for?

In a nutshell, Millennials are looking for 'meaning' in their job, and this is primarily about their ability to grow, develop and expand their skill base. In fact, four out of every 10 members of Gen Y (41%) say that personal growth/advancement is the main reason they choose one job over another, compared to just 25% of Baby Boomers. And, 25% of Gen Y members say that "lack of opportunities for advancement" is the primary reason they would leave their current organization, compared to just 13% of Baby Boomers.

Most importantly however, more than three-quarters of Gen Y members (77%) feel that the ability to excel is fundamental to deriving meaning from their work, compared to just 67% of Baby Boomers and 57% of the Silent Generation. Unfortunately, less than half of Gen Y members (47%) feel that they actually get this 'meaning' from their work. Clearly, something about the way we think about 'growth' and advancement in most organizations simply isn't hitting the mark for Gen Y.

The issues of growth, career paths, workplace responsibility, and promotion, frequently arise for Gen Y. While their Silent Generation and Baby Boomer predecessors had a laser-like focus on the career ladder, the Millennials are intently focused on what Deloitte terms the 'career lattice'—lateral movement, new opportunities, continual development, and intellectual challenge rather than a simple 'climb to the top.'

Here's where life gets complicated.

This will shock many seasoned organizational leaders, but this focus on meaning requires managers to manage. It requires them to manage individuals, not just tasks. And, frankly, many of our managers haven't figured out how to do this yet. Actually, many of our managers haven't managed in years. In many instances, organizations have stopped asking them to manage and have instead asked them to just 'do'.

This evolution has created a major issue for organizations seeking to motivate the newest members of their workforce. If we're looking at a generation that is seeking meaning in their work, and we know that meaning is different for everyone, managers need to be encouraged to understand what that 'meaning' looks like for everyone on their team. This is going to put the focus back on the ways that managers do their jobs, and it's going to require HR to provide significant support to help managers develop a tailored, yet consistent, approach that actually works for Gen Y (as well as everyone else).

Performance indicators and work-in-progress meetings keep the focus on the tasks that people are doing, and while this is obviously important on one level, it doesn't address the issue of motivating Gen Y employees to do their best work at an individual level.

"

IN THEIR WORDS

A manager is more of a consultant in a way. It is important to keep things exciting and different. We get bored easily and while there are tedious things that have to be done, it's the projects that let us use our imaginations and create our own ideas that keep us interested."

RECENT GRADUATE, MIDWEST USA

Members of Gen Y are loyal to their career or professions first—organizations come second. For companies focused on just-in-time talent supply chains, this works well. So, the effective leader will take the time to understand what motivates and inspires the Gen Y employee and will will use that knowledge when devising motivating and challenging work or tasks.

In addition to creating these career-building challenges, effective managers will also be mindful of the need to demonstrate to Gen Y workers that their contribution is valued.

We found that younger workers were significantly more likely to believe that they should be rewarded or recognized in some way for a job well done than their older colleagues. In fact, according to the *2012 Kelly Global Workforce Index*, just 11% of members of Gen Ys said "no reward" is necessary for a job well done, compared to 19% of Baby Boomers and 30% of the Silent Generation.

NO REWARD IS REQUIRED FOR A JOB WELL DONE (% YES)

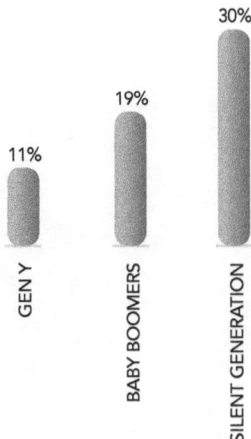

30%

19%

11%

GEN Y

BABY BOOMERS

SILENT GENERATION

PERSONAL GROWTH/ ADVANCEMENT IS THE MAIN REASON TO CHOOSE ONE JOB OVER ANOTHER (% YES)

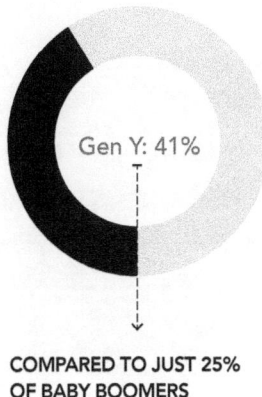

Gen Y: 41%

COMPARED TO JUST 25% OF BABY BOOMERS

But it's important to see this need for reward in context. Gen Y workers want reinforcement, not because they're impatient, needy and self-centered, but because they're looking for signposts that tell them they're on the right path, and that you approve of how they're progressing. This is a subtle, but profound, difference.

The Gen Y mindset is more about the journey than the destination. It's about what's happening right where they're already standing, rather than what might be promised further down the road. They aren't necessarily interested in a decades-long career with your company, but they are very focused on interesting and challenging work that will stretch/grow their skillset this quarter.

HOW EMPLOYERS CAN RESPOND

Communicate the big picture, reward the small wins: Gen Y wants to know how their work fits with the big strategic picture, just as much as older generations do. However, they require recognition for the steps achieved along the way. Remember, it's a journey for them. Make it worthwhile by providing signposts along the way. HR has been saying that we must treat all employees consistently. But, line managers won't survive with blind obedience, and HR isn't supporting business with this blind assessment. Generation Y is different. And, organizations must adapt to get the most out of this difference. For decades, organizations have been focusing on standardization, and now they need to adapt to do the complete opposite.

Help them excel: Gen Y workers are far more likely to derive 'meaning' from their work by their ability to excel and develop in their field, yet this sometimes has more to do with a career 'lattice' than the career 'ladder.' So, find ways to provide career-building opportunities, even if that doesn't mean an immediate promotion straight away.

GEN Y HEAD:
WHAT ARE
THEY THINKING?

Welcome to the experience economy.
This is where Gen Ys live—and this is
what shapes much of how they think.

In the experience economy, we don't deliver goods or a service, we deliver an experience. This can be *part* of a product or service, but it has a distinct value in, and of, itself.

Just as the act of unpacking your latest i-device is an experience Apple has deliberately 'created', the experience of a workplace must also be deliberately built and delivered on a daily basis. A large percentage of this 'delivery' falls in the lap of the manager/supervisor.

The flow of information, the ease and quality of connections and collaboration, the facilitation of self-expression and feedback—these are all experiences that directly impact the way Gen Y workers feel about their workplace, and their place within it. How are you managing this experience within your department/team? Getting this right for younger workers isn't always easy. It often requires challenging specific traditions and entrenched ways of operating, but it's non-negotiable if building a talent supply chain across this age group is a genuine goal.

Another aspect of the Gen Y mindset is that they are heavily informed and influenced by the opinions of those that they trust—and this increasingly includes total strangers. It's not naiveté that drives this, it's their ability and desire to connect with people based on similar interests and ways of operating.

66

IN THEIR WORDS

I don't want to sit around and wait for a bunch of other stuff to happen. I'm all about taking as much or as little time as needed to get something done, and do it well. There is no need for wasted time."

MARKETING SPECIALIST, MIDWEST USA

Our research—empirical, experiential and anecdotal—suggests that Gen Y may have the most highly refined BS detectors ever. In fact, one of the Gen Y workers we spoke to said this about the way her generation interacts with the proliferation of information and messages from advertisers, employers, media and everything in between: "We are so overwhelmed with different sources of information, particularly advertising, that we tend to ignore it as much as possible. Being able to get information from a variety of sources has taught us to not trust the direct source, or not only talk to one person. If we hear it from multiple places, we are more likely to believe it."

Ignore this advice at your peril. Members of Gen Y are far less likely to believe what you say unless they can verify it independently via other sources. Trying to hide, ignore or gloss over negative media coverage or customer feedback about your organization's activities or products is a sure-fire recipe for disengagement and distrust. Gone are the days when the CEO could put out an internal statement (written by the PR department) about an issue in the media and expect the workforce to accept it. Organizations now need to engage in dialogue about negative media coverage or contentious internal issues—'motherhood statements' and platitudes simply will not suffice.

"

IN THEIR WORDS
_____

We need a free environment, where once the work is allotted, and a timeframe decided, we should be left alone. But, we should be given the confidence that we can come back to the supervisors for a solution if we get stuck."

EXECUTIVE RECRUITER GURGAON, INDIA

Members of Gen Y make it their business to seek out people they trust and relate to. They don't always assume this will be their direct manager. They take personal responsibility for finding information and people through their networks—and this can sometimes be misconstrued as undermining authority, or an inability to work within assumed processes. But often, that's not it at all.

'Thinking' and 'experiencing' are what Gen Y workers are good at. And sometimes this just makes everyone else a little bit uncomfortable. Keep in mind, if you allow them to use their strength in this area, it just might lead to an innovative approach or experience that your internal team would have never considered. Diversity of thought and diversity of networking is what they bring to the table.

HOW EMPLOYERS CAN RESPOND

Evaluate the experience of working at your organization: This doesn't always mean adding services within the building such as dry cleaners and bowling alleys, but it might. As long as the experience reflects your brand and has clear links back to productivity, engagement and talent retention, nothing is a dumb idea. Ask your Gen Y employees what changes they would like to see in their workplace. Chances are, if they are involved with the ideation, it will stick and make a difference. When in doubt, ask.

Find ways to promote positive dialogue about generational issues: Where you sit in the organizational hierarchy dictates where you stand. In other words, it's difficult for the generations to know and understand why they have different approaches and values unless they get to know each other. Providing specific forums where the issues of not just managing, but understanding, the needs and approaches of the generations will help to bridge the divide. Training courses may be part of the solution, but also finding ways to enable different generational perspectives to be discussed by the individuals themselves is just as important.

THE WORKPLACE COLLISION

From the traditional employer point of view, work hasn't changed all that much in the past five or six decades. Work is work, and that's how it will be for the foreseeable future—just as soon as younger generations get with the status quo, that is.

But the reality is, that work has changed, the workplace has changed, and so has the workforce. The progressive employer already understands this. The problem is, they are in the minority. The traditional employer, then, sees EVOLUTION.

As far as the Millennial sees it, work is in flux, just as the rest of the world is. Nothing is stable, static or long-term, nor should it be. Here's a staggering thought—the redefined workforce has redefined the workplace. And they dig it. So, Gen Y sees REVOLUTION.

And here we have the makings of a great (perhaps perceived) productivity collision.

WORK AS THE TRADITIONAL EMPLOYER SEES IT	WORK AS THE MILLENNIAL SEES IT
The office	The Third Place
Offices to cubicles, back to offices again	Laptops, iPads and iPhones. All information you need is on the internet, and working is 24/7, not 9–5
From suit and tie to business casual (and at some firms, back again)	Self-expression, not conformity. The person and their outcomes, not the clothing or title
Flexibility is required, but not ideal. It's harder to manage large volumes of people telecommuting, job sharing etc.	They chose their classes and timetables and submitted assignments online, now they choose where to work and submit work via VPNs. It's not just practical, it's more efficient
'Face time' means meetings in the office	'Face time' means Apple 'Facetime', messaging, virtual collaboration
The attitude of workers is changing work (not always for the better)	The changing nature of work requires a new way of working
Fear of loss of control	Question the effectiveness of, and need for, traditional, hierarchical control
Clear distinction between 'work' and 'not work'	Blurred line between 'work' and 'personal lives'
Social networking leads to decreased capacity and productivity	Social networking is capacity-building and leads to innovation/ better perspective
An inability to adapt to the current structures is due to immaturity, lack of discipline and avoidance of doing the hard yards	Adapting to current organizational structures is a waste of time because they don't make sense

CONCLUSION

Managers and organizations have a new challenge. Instead of managing Gen Y workers, they need to deeply study what makes them tick—something they've been resisting for far
too long already.

Rather than hoping Gen Y workers are simply going to grow up and realize their older colleagues were right all along, leaders need to understand that the differences are
here to stay. They're hard-wired and fundamental to the way members of Gen Y live
and work—and understanding them is now non-negotiable (if you understand global workforce demographics).

Members of Gen Y value connection and rely on networks. They seek dialogue and input regardless of location, rank or role. They search for meaning and the ability to excel—and they want to be rewarded when they're heading in the right direction. They take personal responsibility for finding the information and people they need to do their job, and this makes for a big challenge for most traditional organizations and hierarchies. It's just not how we do things...yet.

Lurking within all this misunderstanding is a huge opportunity.

Thinking and experiencing are what members of Gen Y are good at. And, if you allow them to use their strengths in these areas, it just might lead to a new, innovative approach or experience that would otherwise never have been considered. After all, innovation, creativity, collaboration and flexibility are the very characteristics that many organizations are striving to increase, right?

Diversity of thought is what Gen Y workers bring to the table, and as long as leaders learn to understand and harness its value, there is a light at the end of the tunnel for organizations experiencing the bitter divide we all know as 'the generation gap.'

The choice is yours. You can continue managing Gen Y workers, but for the leader who wants to harness their full potential, it's time to #understandgeny.

SOURCE MATERIALS

1. 'Gen Y Speaks Out About Performance Reviews' Colette Martin http://www.forbes.com/sites/work-in-progress/2011/07/15/gen-y-speaks-out-on-performance-reviews/
2. 2011 Kelly Global Workforce Index
3. 2012 Kelly Global Workforce Index
4. 'The Conference Board CEO Challenge® 2012: Risky Business—Focusing on Innovation and Talent in a Volatile World: March 2012', Charles Mitchell, Rebecca L. Ray, Ph.D. and Bart van Ark.
5. The Cisco Connected World Technology Report, September 2011
6. 'Fear of Missing Out (FOMO)', JWT, March 2012 Update
7. 'Millennials at Work: reshaping the workplace', PwC, 2011
8. Generation Y Around The World, Pieter Van Vuyst and Joeri Van de Bergh, Insites Consulting
9. 'Gen Z Digital in their DNA', JWT, Will Palley, April 2012

THE LEADERSHIP DEFICIT

Recruiting and Retaining the
Multi-generational Workforce

@JASONSMORGA AND @LANCEJRICHARDS

CONTENTS

PAGE 40   Introduction

PAGE 42   The Aging and Declining Workforce

PAGE 52   Four Generations: A Call for Workplace Agility

PAGE 60   The Growth of Free Agency

PAGE 66   Managing generational diversity

PAGE 74   Success Stories

PAGE 80   Conclusion

PAGE 81   References

BUSINESSES EVERYWHERE ARE GRAPPLING WITH AN **UNFOLDING SKILLS DILEMMA** THAT IS CHALLENGING THE WAY WE MANAGE AND PLAN THE WORKFORCE OF THE FUTURE.

People are remaining in the workforce longer than they used to, yet there is a growing shortage of skilled talent. The aging and declining workforce is a global phenomenon taking place in all industries and across traditional boundaries.

Generational differences, which emerged over the last decade are beginning to solidify and have lasting implications for the management of human capital.

In addition, the rise of a new breed of self-employed 'free agents' is injecting a volatile element into the mix which is forcing employers to reassess the way they select, deploy and interact with staff.

How do companies prepare for and manage these trends? What are the keys to success as the workforce continues to evolve?

This paper explains why talent is dwindling, and paints a detailed picture of the profile of those that comprise the contemporary workforce. It discusses the challenges employers face, and offers suggestions for recruiting and retaining top talent, as well as casting a spotlight on companies that are tackling these challenges in innovative ways.

LANCE JENSEN RICHARDS, GPHR, SPHR

JASON S. MORGA, PHR

THE AGING AND
DECLINING WORKFORCE

Evolutionary shifts in the workforce are to be expected as the world changes. But today's global workforce is undergoing an unprecedented transition—as companies everywhere are faced with recruiting and retaining top talent from a labor force that is shrinking overall, yet includes increasing numbers of older workers.

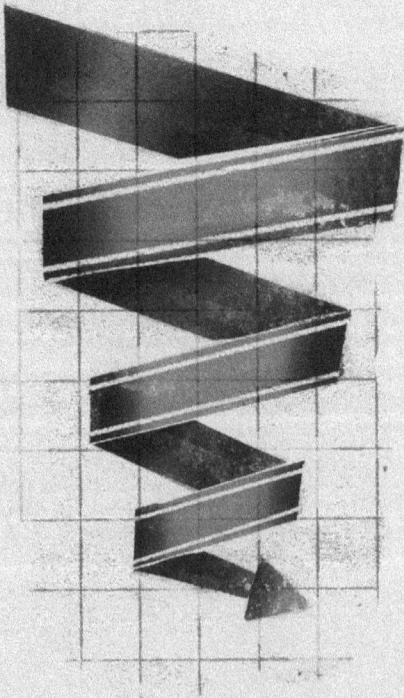

Longevity by the Numbers

In all countries, people are living longer and working longer. Advances in medical technology have improved health care and lowered mortality rates. As a result, people over age 50 constitute a larger part of the overall population, and a larger part of the global workforce.

Governments around the world are beginning to take notice and take steps to adapt to an aging workforce. More than one million French workers took to the streets in the latter part of 2010 to protest the government's plans to overhaul pensions and raise the retirement age from 60 to 62. In the United States, the median age of workers has risen from 34 to 40 in the past 30 years.

Since 1980, the percentage of workers aged 50 and above in the United States has risen from 26 percent of the population to 37 percent. And by 2050, the share of workers aged 55 and older is expected to reach 19.1 percent, up from just over 14 percent in 2002 (see Figure 1).

But although a multi-generational labor pool presents challenges, it can also offer benefits. Organizations can capitalize on this new workforce by developing targeted strategies for managing generational segments of the talent pool in order to harness the unique contributions of each group.

FIGURE 1.
The Aging Workforce

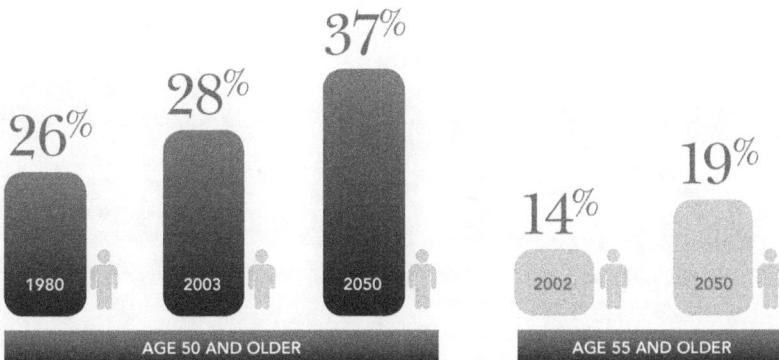

26%	28%	37%
1980	2003	2050
AGE 50 AND OLDER		

14%	19%
2002	2050
AGE 55 AND OLDER	

From a demographic standpoint, 'prime-aged' workers are 25 to 54 years old. This group has grown significantly over the past two decades, but in recent years, has flattened and is now declining. Meanwhile, the older workforce has been steadily creeping higher.

Since December 2007, the number of prime-aged workers in the U.S labor force has declined by 0.7 percent, while the number of workers over the age of 55 has increased by 7.6 percent. In fact, the number of workers aged 55 and older is higher now than any time since 1948 (see Figure 2).

What is behind this shift in the labor market, and why is the pool of top talent shrinking? The retirement of Baby Boomers is the leading factor behind projected labor shortages, leaving fewer numbers of skilled workers. And with technology advancing at a rapid pace, the need for skilled workers is increasing at an exponential rate around the world. Unfortunately, the numbers of college graduates is not keeping pace with what the global workforce requires.

FIGURE 2.

Demographic workforce trends

Employment level by age group, Jan 1948–Aug 2009

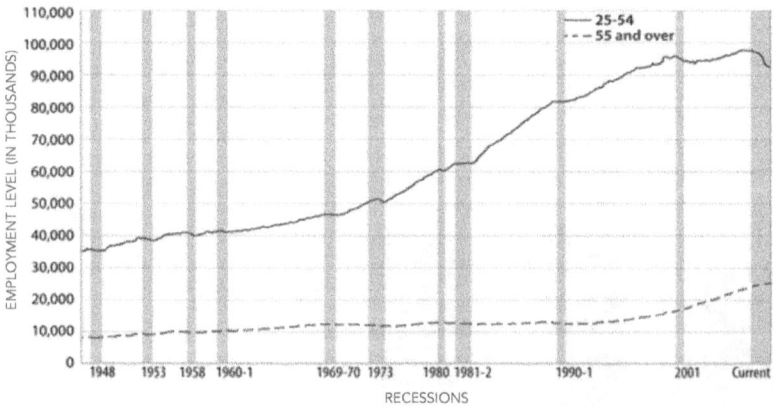

Shaded bars indicate recessions as defined by the National Bureau of Economic Research.
Source: Bureau of Labor Statistics Popuation Survey.

In theory, there should be an abundance of skilled workers flooding the labor pool, because attendance at colleges and universities is at an all-time high. But attending is one thing—graduating is another, with completion rates at only 58 percent.

There are fewer young people graduating because there are fewer young people.

The Shock Heard Round the World

Many countries are feeling the pinch and seeing unprecedented changes to demographics and workforce trends. In European Union, the number of people aged 20 to 59 years is expected to decrease by nearly 25 percent by 2050, while the number of people over the age of 60 will climb by nearly 50 percent.

Japan is a prime example of the gravity of these statistics. In 2007, some 21 percent of the Japanese population was older than age 65; by 2055, that will rise to more than 40 percent. During this time, the population of Japan is projected to shrink from nearly 128 million to 95 million.

In Japan, biology is shaping destiny at a frightening pace. More Japanese women are working, so they are marrying and having children later in life, while more than 30 percent of Japanese women aged 30 and older are not married. The value system of many Japanese women has changed considerably, bringing a structural shift in the country's demographic make-up.

The imbalance between supply and demand is further complicated by fertility rate issues. As Figure 3 shows, there are simply too few children being born in developed countries.

The total fertility rate (TFR) is a measure of the number of births per woman in the population and serves as a proxy for population growth. A rate of 2.1 children per woman is generally considered the replacement rate. Above this rate a population is increasing and below, it is generally falling.

FIGURE 3.
Global fertility rates, present and future

TOTAL FERTILITY IN 2005–2010, MEDIUM VARIANT (CHILDREN PER WOMAN)

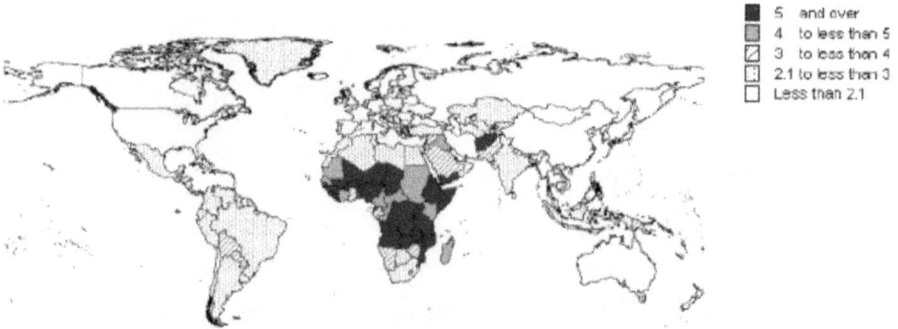

5   and over
4   to less than 5
3   to less than 4
2.1 to less than 3
Less than 2.1

Source: Population Division of the Department of Economic and Social Affairs of the United Nations
Secretariat (2007). World Population Prospects: The 2006 Revision, Highlights. New York: United Nations.
NOTE: The boundaries shown on this map do not imply official endorsement or acceptance by the
United Nations.

TOTAL FERTILITY IN 2045–2050, MEDIUM VARIANT (CHILDREN PER WOMAN)

5   and over
4   to less than 5
3   to less than 4
2.1 to less than 3
Less than 2.1

Source: Population Division of the Department of Economic and Social Affairs of the United Nations
Secretariat (2007). World Population Prospects: The 2006 Revision, Highlights. New York: United Nations.
NOTE: The boundaries shown on this map do not imply official endorsement or acceptance by the
United Nations.

FIGURE 4.

Fertility rates in major areas: Past, present, and potential future

Major area	1970–1975	2005–2010	Low	Medium	High	Constant
			Total fertility (children per woman)			
			2045–2050			
World	4.47	2.55	1.54	2.02	2.51	3.49
More developed regions	2.13	1.60	1.29	1.79	2.28	1.68
Less developed regions	5.41	2.75	1.57	2.05	2.54	3.69
Least developed countries	6.61	4.63	2.02	2.50	2.99	5.49
Other less developed countries	5.25	2.45	1.42	1.91	2.41	3.07
Africa	6.72	4.67	1.97	2.46	2.95	5.47
Asia	5.04	2.34	1.40	1.90	2.39	2.94
Europe	2.16	1.45	1.26	1.76	2.26	1.47
Latin America and the Caribbean	5.04	2.37	1.36	1.86	2.36	2.67
Northern America	2.01	2.00	1.35	1.85	2.35	1.99
Oceania	3.23	2.30	1.43	1.93	2.43	2.83

Source: Population Division of the Department of Economic and Social Affairs of the United Nations Secretariat (2007). World Population Prospects: The 2006 Revision, Highlights. New York: United Nations.

Countries such as South Korea, Italy, and Germany have fertility levels at alarmingly low levels. South Korea's fertility rate is less than half the replacement rate, 1.08; Japan's is slightly higher at 1.26. It's only in developing countries where fertility rates are at abundant levels – for instance, Nigeria at 4.91, and Guatemala at 3.47. The problem is that the higher fertility rates in developing countries do not balance out the shortage in developed countries, because developing countries simply do not have the educational infrastructure to convert these newborns into skilled workers.

The fertility rate in the United States was hovering around 2.05 in 2005, having risen from a low of 1.74 in 1976, but still not quite at replacement level. According to a 2006 United Nations study, from 2005 to 2010, 73 countries had fertility rates below the replacement level, whereas 122 countries had fertility levels at or above that rate. Among those, the fertility levels were at or above 5 children per woman in 27 countries— 25 of which are the least developed (see Figure 4).

FIGURE 5.
Global demographic and social trends

The current European Union (EU) nations face shrinking labor pools.*

• The number of people aged 20–59 years will decrease from **208.7M in 2000** to **151.2M in 2050.**

• During the same period, the number of people over the age of 60 will climb from 82.1 million to 125.1 million.

Central and South America: high fertility rates and high levels of unemployment, in addition to northern migration.

South Africa: skilled labor shortage; unskilled labor surplus.

Sub-Saharan Africa: labor shortage predominantly in agriculture.

East Africa (i.e., Eritrea): skilled workers shortage.

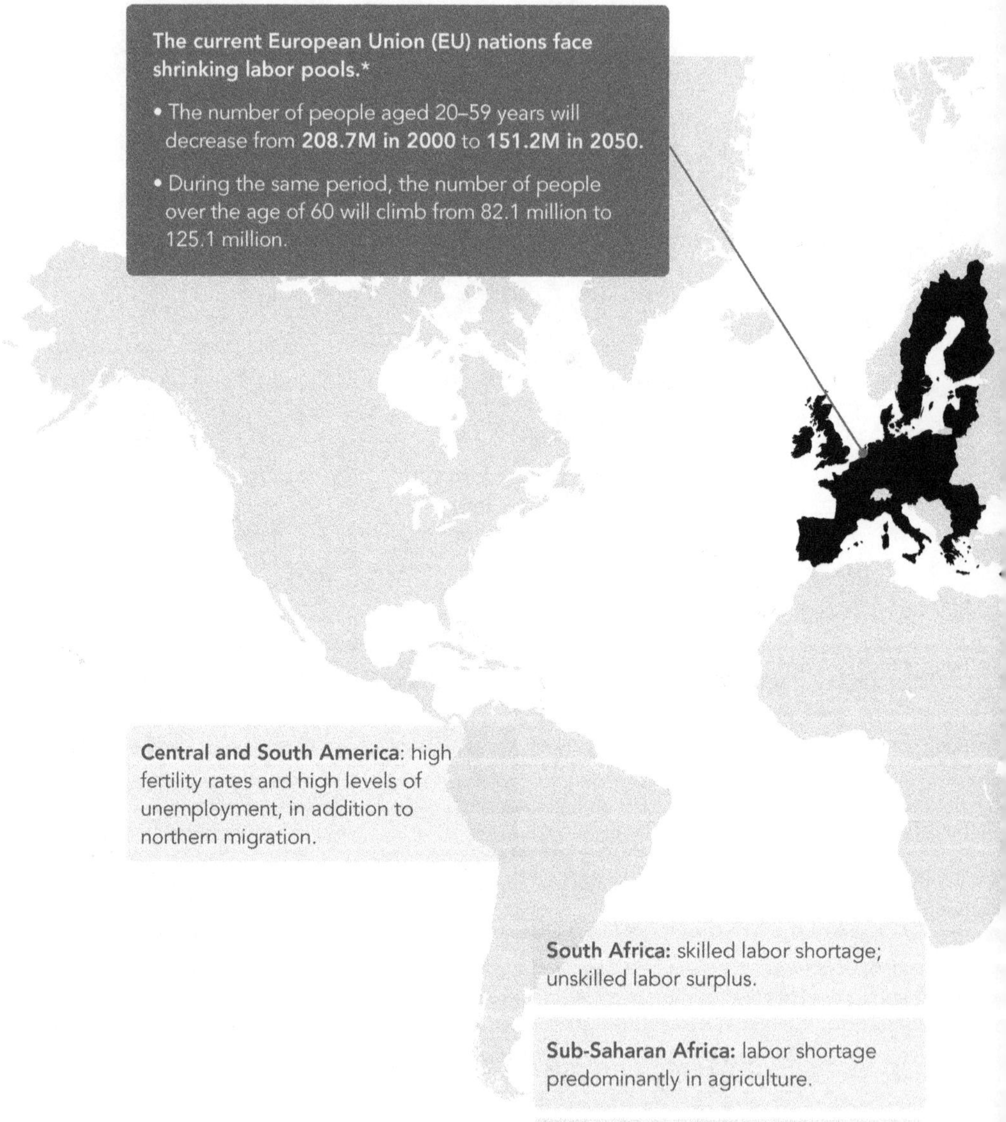

Source: EU Information – Demographic and Social Trends Issue Paper. Europe's Changing Demography Constraints and Bottlenecks. Fact Sheet: Living Happily Ever After. The Economic Implications of Aging Societies. Watson Wyatt Worldwide & World Economic Forum. No data provided.

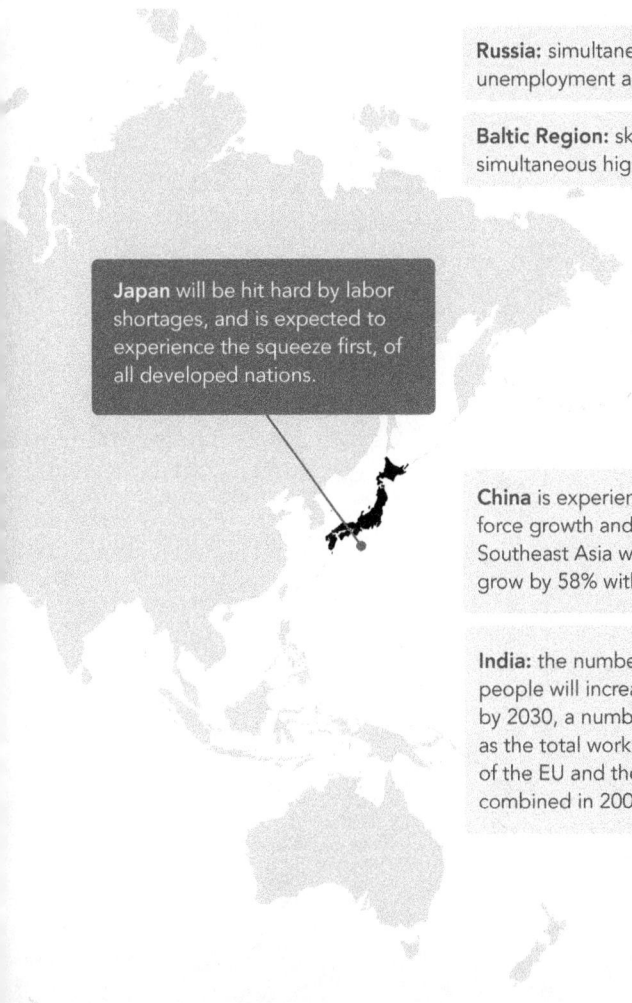

Russia: simultaneous high unemployment and skills shortage.

Baltic Region: skills shortage and simultaneous high unemployment.

Japan will be hit hard by labor shortages, and is expected to experience the squeeze first, of all developed nations.

China is experiencing both rapid labor force growth and a skills shortage. Southeast Asia will see its workforce grow by 58% within the next 30 years.

India: the number of working-age people will increase by 335 million by 2030, a number almost as large as the total working-age population of the EU and the United States combined in 2000.*

Australia: expects a shortage of 500,000 workers by 2020.

New Zealand: already has shortages of skilled workers in local building and manufacturing industries. (Local PR).

Even if there were a sudden, miraculous rise in fertility rates, the effects wouldn't be =felt for decades. Babies born today will take a minimum of 22 years before they enter the workforce.

Yet in the developing world where birth rates are increasing, there will be equally perverse outcomes. Southeast Asia will likely see its workforce grow by 58 percent within the next 30 years. China is experiencing rapid labor force growth, but a significant lack of skilled labor. In India, the number of working-aged people will increase by 335 million by 2030— a number almost as large as the total working-aged population of the EU and the United States combined in 2000.

What this means is that in the developing world, there is a growing surplus of unskilled labor, at the same time as demand for unskilled labor is declining. It's precisely the flip side of the problem in the developed world, where there is a growing shortage of skilled workers at a time when their need for skilled labor is becoming greater.

With the overall workforce aging, birth rates in mature markets dropping, labor pools in developed nations shrinking, the numbers of skilled workers dropping, and the demand for skilled workers accelerating along with technology evolutions—the global workforce could soon be in a world of trouble. Figure 5 gives an idea of what is looming.

Navigating the Challenges of a Workforce in Transition

These trends pose major challenges for individuals, businesses and indeed for nations. Many emerging economies simply do not have the ability to educate the populations they are producing. From an HR perspective, this trend may be irreversible. Already, high fertility rates and high levels of unemployment are significantly impacting the labor force in Central and South America. Even if steps could be taken now to build stronger education systems, it would still take decades to have any positive impact on the supply of skilled workers and middle managers in the global labor force. The problem from a global labor force perspective is that the countries that are the best equipped to educate people today, have the lowest birth rates.

We're not running out of people—we're running out of talent

Specific industries such as IT and healthcare are beginning to be significantly impacted by the dwindling availability of skilled labor. Workers with valuable skills are in demand and often leave their jobs to accept more lucrative offers, leaving behind vacancies that may be impossible to fill. A 2003 World Health Organization study of six African countries revealed that most health workers plan to migrate for higher salaries.

Bettering their take-home pay is great for individual workers, but hard on the communities they leave behind. When a doctor in Ghana leaves a position that pays $300 a month to move to the United States to accept a job as a nurse making $4,500 a month, an American town gains a very skilled nurse—but a village in Ghana loses a doctor.

Sometimes the imbalances that exist in the labor market are 'corrected' in ways that might appear plausible from a strict economic perspective, but which come at a terrible social cost.

FOUR GENERATIONS: A CALL FOR WORKPLACE AGILITY

A multi-generational workforce requires a trans-generational solution. For the first time, employers are challenged by the phenomenon of four distinct generations coming together in the workplace simultaneously. Each generation has its own unique attitudes toward work, and those diverse approaches often result in intergenerational conflict.

Generational differences may pose challenges for employers who want to get optimal performance from their entire workforce. Yet the diversity of experience and knowledge offered by four distinct generational mindsets can provide tangible benefits if managed well. The challenge for employers is to embrace the talent mix, tap into it, and use its strengths to deliver operational performance.

The Silent Generation—The Traditionalists

The Silent Generation is the segment of the population born between 1925 and 1945. The label was coined in a 1951 Time article about young people coming of age, who were born during the Great Depression and World War II. Almost two-thirds are married and 29 percent are widowed or divorced. Three-quarters are grandparents, and 26 percent earned a post-graduate degree. The technologies this generation developed included radio, movies, radar, and instant cameras, and these innovations laid the groundwork for many technological advances in the late 20th century.

They are usually the parents of Baby Boomers, and they value hard work, dedication, respect for authority, conformity, and adherence to rules. The work ethic of the Silent Generation was built around responsibility and long-term commitment, so they usually prefer the status quo and can be slow to embrace change. This generation of workers shared common experiences of hardships, war, and socioeconomic conflicts. Some even remember living through the Great Depression as children. For most of them, the experiences they shared and the challenges they faced brought a sense of camaraderie that subsequent generations have never experienced in quite the same way.

Baby Boomers—The 'Me' Generation

Baby Boomers were born following World War II, between 1946 and 1964
—a time that was marked by a 'booming' increase in birth rates.
Baby Boomers are generally associated with rejecting or redefining
traditional values in favor of personal gratification. Most are married, many
have been married more than once, and one-third are grandparents.
Seventy-seven percent of all Boomers are employed, and two-thirds work
full-time. They are a highly educated group, with 39 percent having earned
a post-graduate degree. Technological advances that these workers
can take credit for include the microwave, VCRs, hand-held calculators,
computers, color televisions, and credit cards. Many Boomers have
delayed their retirement; 80 percent will continue to work as contractors or
free agents part-time or part of the year.

Having grown up in a time of affluence, Baby Boomers are optimistic and
genuinely expect society to improve over time. Their developmental years
were marked by many turbulent times including the Cold War, the civil
rights movement, women's liberation, and political assassinations.
A common bond that they came to depend upon was the emergence of
music as a regular part of life and society.

Pursuit of personal growth is a key goal of Baby Boomers, who are
often called the 'me' or 'ageless' generation. They are independent,
over-achieving mult-itaskers who work long hours and struggle with
balancing their life and work. Statistics show that they really care about
the future of their companies, and they are loyal, strong performers. Kelly
Services® data shows that Boomers who work as free agents or temporary
contractors on assignment have a higher retention rate than their younger
cohorts. They typically work 22 percent more hours than workers from
other generations, average 3.32 years tenure with employers, and receive
94 percent positive feedback ratings from customers.

Generation X—The Bridge Generation

Generation X is the generation born after the end of the baby boom. Sometimes called the 'Baby Busters,' demographers usually define this group as people born between 1961 and 1981, and they are small in number compared to the generations before and after them. Nearly two-thirds are parents, one-third are working parents, and the divorce rate among Gen X workers is nearly 50 percent. This is the best educated generation in the workforce today, with more than 40 percent having earned a college degree or higher. They tend to reject authority and embrace risk, and are willing to jump from job to job to pursue growth and opportunity. Gen X workers are self-reliant, techno-literate, global thinkers—and they place a high value on working to live, rather than living to work.

Considered a 'bridge' generation, Gen X workers typically demand short-term payoffs with immediate feedback and rewards for a job well done. They are interested in climbing the corporate ladder, but can be cynical and frustrated by tradition. They often question hierarchy, formal authority, and traditional institutions, preferring to have more control over their time and their future. They are the first to blur the lines between the workplace and home, and they have brought about workplace changes such as telecommuting and on-site child care. Gen Xers do not value the same things Baby Boomers considered to be important, so employers should not expect management styles used for Boomers to work well with Gen X.

The developmental years of Gen X were marked by economic stagnation, with serious societal developments such as the AIDS crisis, increasing poverty, rising divorce rates, and moms going back to work. Gen X workers grew up with MTV and cable television, and are intimately familiar with technological innovations such as floppy disks, personal computers, cell phones, DVD, and e-mail. For Xers, computers have always been a part of their lives. But because PC networks and the Internet didn't exist in their early years, this group became a group of technically apt people working independently. Although group interactions in person decreased, computers and cell phones still made it possible for Xers to collaborate— only in different ways than ever before.

Generation Y—The Millennials

Generation Y, also dubbed Generation Next or Echo Boomers, is now entering the workforce at a rapid pace, and there are about 70 million of them. Most demographers suggest that this generation was born between 1982 and the turn of the millennium. Nearly a third are currently attending a college or university, and their parents, family, religion, and generosity are of central importance. They display a high tolerance toward other cultures and lifestyles, and they volunteer in their communities more than prior generations did. Gen Yers join organizations and causes not because they have to, but because they want to—because they want to contribute to something significant. They are moral and committed, and they value personal achievement.

Often called the Millennials, Gen Y workers are definitely a different breed. Ambitious and demanding, they question everything and need constant feedback at work because they get it in every other aspect of their lives. If they don't see a good reason for working late or making a long commute, they usually won't do it. Loyalty to one company is not their strong suit, although they are generally very loyal to their profession and the people they work with. In a recent survey of Millennials, nearly all of the respondents said that having 'meaning' in their work was of utmost importance. But when asked if they were actually getting meaning out of their work, only about a quarter of them said they were. So there is an enormous disconnection here.

Gen Y is the largest consumer group in history. Although they grew up in a time of economic prosperity, Gen Y workers have experienced life-defining events such as school violence and terrorism. The technological expertise of these hipsters has been influenced by the rapid growth of the Internet, iPods®, smart phones, text messaging, high-definition TV, and Xbox®/PlayStation® gaming. Their world is smaller than that of any other generation, thanks to technology that has brought the world to them. 'Global' means something entirely different to Gen Y than it did to previous generations. They use iPhones® to talk to people on the other side of the planet, instantaneously. They communicate with each other via e-mail, Skype™, Facebook™, and Twitter™.

Tomorrow's Generation

As Figure 6 below shows, Gen Y alone will represent almost 40 percent of the United States labor force by 2012. In aggregate, Gen X and Gen Y will represent 70 percent of the workforce by 2012.

And there's another generation waiting in the wings to make its debut.

FIGURE 6.

The four generations in today's workforce

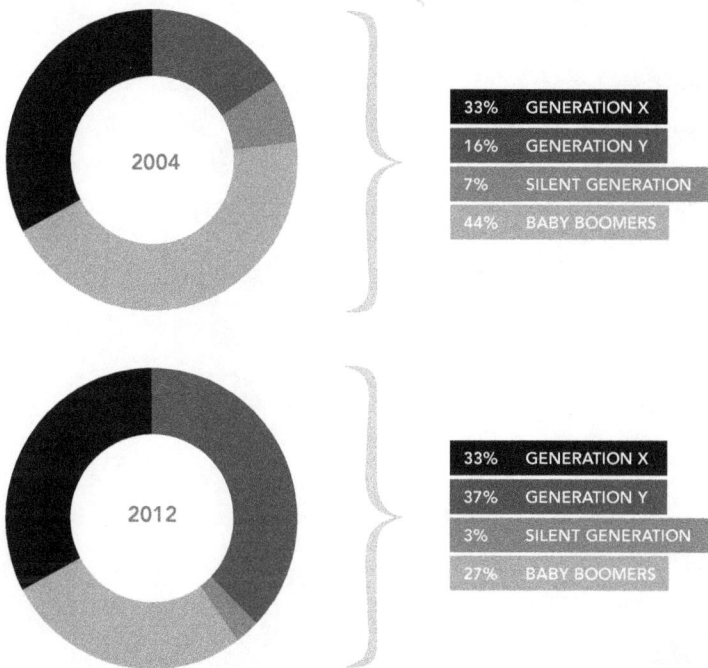

2004	
33%	GENERATION X
16%	GENERATION Y
7%	SILENT GENERATION
44%	BABY BOOMERS

2012	
33%	GENERATION X
37%	GENERATION Y
3%	SILENT GENERATION
27%	BABY BOOMERS

Source: Bureau of Labor Statistics

Generation Z – The Internet Generation

The next generation to hit the labor force will be the most technology-enabled generation yet. Generation Z, children born between 1990 and now, were holding Gameboys® and Leapsters® in their hands at a very early age. They are used to seeing computers in the kitchen; every classroom they have been in had a PC; and they probably started carrying a cell phone by the time they were 12 years old. They have watched their Gen X parents juggling cell phones and smart phones, and they are intimately familiar with texting and instant messaging. Many are likely to spend more time communicating electronically with their parents than sitting at the dinner table talking to them.

As the workforce continues to age and decline, this new generation will turn the supply and demand equation upside down—they will own their employers, and they will make unprecedented demands on the workplace. And, irony of ironies, the Millennials will have to manage them.

Understanding and Managing Generational Challenges

As we've discussed, today's workforce is growing older. Workers aged 55 years and older are expected to comprise 24 percent of the workforce by 2018. More than 78 million Baby Boomers are being followed by a far smaller cohort of only 45 million Gen X workers, so there will be a shrinking pool of prime-aged workers to fill the gaps. The demand for talented Gen X leaders will increase, but the supply will decrease.

Meanwhile, Baby Boomers are staying in the workforce longer, in part because of the beating their pension plans took as a result of the global financial crisis. However, although the growing trend of delaying retirement is slowing down the exit of Boomers from the workplace, there will still be a significant deficit in leadership and the competition for older, more experienced leaders will intensify.

Unique trends are developing due to upheavals in the workforce. Younger workers are shifting their sights away from traditional career paths that involve loyalty to a single company for long tenures. Instead, they are assuming more responsibility earlier in their careers and focusing on developing skills that will make them marketable to multiple employers.

Differences in work ethics and values will continue to escalate as the age spectrum in our workforce becomes more pronounced. As a result, organizations will be forced to rethink, revamp, and adapt their recruiting, retention, and training strategies.

THE GROWTH OF
FREE AGENCY

Throughout the last decade, a strong trend
has emerged toward building more flexible,
project-based workforces. This trend began
long before the current recession, largely
because modern technology has made it
possible for people to connect and work
together from wherever they are.

One of the most important workforce trends of the past two decades has been the rise of the new breed of independent free agents – consultants, freelancers, contractors and 'micropreneurs'.

Free agents are not traditional '9 to 5' employees working for one employer. They are untethered, independent professionals or consultants, temporary or contract employees, and they move from project to project, location to location. They span all ages, professions, incomes, and educational levels, and they are interested in working for themselves. Free agents prioritize freedom and flexibility over the security of traditional employment models, and they are always keeping an eye out for more interesting or rewarding assignments that afford the best work/life balance.

Many of these are professionals who have been dislodged from salaried careers as a consequence of business restructuring and economic upheaval. They may have been laid-off from well-paid full time jobs in 1990s recession or the most recent global downturn. Instead of waiting for new opportunities to come to them, they have started up their own businesses, providing labor or services to clients on a project-by-project basis.

Free agency can take many forms, ranging from the freelancer to the entrepreneur or business owner, working as a sole operator, or working with a small staff. Whichever way it is defined, the growth in this form of employment has been remarkable.

The Kelly Services Employment Trends Survey undertaken in early 2011 shows that the percentage of the U.S. population that describes themselves as free agents has virtually doubled from 26 percent in 2008 to 44 percent in 2011. Meanwhile the proportion which is directly employed has fallen from 74 percent to 56 percent over the same period.

FIGURE 7.
Growth of free agents in U.S. population

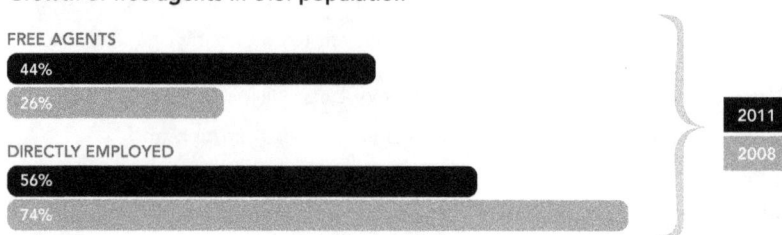

FREE AGENTS
44%
26%

DIRECTLY EMPLOYED
56%
74%

2011
2008

Source: Kelly® Employment Trends Survey, 2011

The survey shows that the vast majority (87 percent) operate without any staff. What is also clear is that the rise of this form of employment has been directly related to global economic conditions. When downturns hit the economy, many of those who are laid off or who have been adversely impacted have little choice but to let their entrepreneurial instincts kick in and embark of some form of self-employment.

The percentage of those who became free agents because of "not being able to find work elsewhere" doubled since 2008. The number that chose free agency because they were terminated or laid off tripled over the same period.

03. THE GROWTH OF FREE AGENCY

FIGURE 8.

Primary reasons for working as a free agent

FLEXIBILITY THAT 'FREE AGENT' WORK OFFERS
19%

FREEDOM THAT 'FREE AGENT' WORK OFFERS
16%

CANNOT FIND WORK ELSEWHERE
10%

TERMINATED/LAID OFF FROM PREVIOUS JOB
10%

MORE WORK/LIFE BALANCE
6%

WORK AS AN ENTREPRENEUR
6%

MORE FLEXIBLE WORKPLACE/WORK FROM HOME
5%

MORE MONEY
5%

MORE EMPOWERMENT/BE OWN BOSS
4%

TIRED OF WORKING FOR AN EMPLOYER
4%

MORE CONTROL OF CAREER
3%

MORE OPPORTUNITIES
3%

FAMILY CONCERNS
3%

TRY SOMETHING NEW
2%

DON'T KNOW/REFUSED
1%

WANTED LESS STRESS
1%

REDUCE RISK/VULNERABILITY
0%

Source: Kelly® Employment Trends Survey, 2011

Yet the main factors that drive the growth of free agency are not solely economic and have much to do with a desire to enjoy a degree of freedom and flexibility not afforded in a traditional employment relationship.

The reasons that people give for becoming free agents reveal much about the collective thinking that is evident across the workforce as a whole. It reflects a desire to be in command of one's 'self', to be able to participate in meaningful work, and to be rewarded in a way that reflects the effort and quality of the input.

When asked about the criteria they used to determine which projects they take-on, the largest percentage of free agents said that they choose a job based on the type of work on offer and their interest in it. In effect, they choose projects that are of interest to them; presumably those that will keep them engaged; that will spur an added effort; that will produce a better quality outcome, and perhaps attract some price premium.

The rise of the free agency phenomenon has also had benefits for those enterprises that use contract or temporary labor. Free agency allows employers to react more quickly to the dynamics of business by being able to expand and contract their workforce according to changing needs. Employers can adopt a just-in-time workforce strategy to save money and streamline processes by maintaining a staff of core personnel responsible for day-to-day operations. When project needs increase or special skill sets are needed, the firm can quickly bring in contractors with the specific skill sets needed. Instead of spending time creating new staff positions and sourcing job candidates, managers can ramp up or scale down according to workflow.

Riding Out the Storm

These distinct shifts in the global workforce—demographic changes, a shortage of talent, the growing empowerment of skilled employees, and the rise of free agents —have converged into a perfect storm for recruiters and managers. The challenge for HR, then, is to develop hiring strategies that attract and keep the most talented people. Because job candidates are also consumers, organizations may want to consider capturing their attention using the same tools used in consumer marketing:

- Attract talent with a strong brand message targeted to specific people.

- Engage talent by offering a recruiting experience that supports the brand message.

- Retain talent in the workplace by validating the promises of the brand message.

Some analysts have said that today's global economy is transitioning to a knowledge economy, where skills and expertise are a valuable commodity for organizations—just as important as economic resources. Because of the shifting dynamics of the workforce, companies are moving away from a focus on cost and speed to focus on the quality of each hire. They are willing to accept higher costs and slower results, as long as they get the right skills.

Companies depend on innovation to be successful. And talent innovates.

MANAGING GENERATIONAL DIVERSITY

The task of managing the generational mix
in the workplace for maximum efficiency
is one of the most challenging facing
managers and business owners today.

The mix of different generations and their associated aspirations, together with the rise of a more entrepreneurial class of free agents is re-shaping the way that businesses operate, and the way employees are engaged and deployed.

In trying to unravel the complexity around this new era in human capital, Kelly Services has, since 2008, been surveying a large sample of individuals from around the globe to gain insights into their thinking about work and career. The Kelly Global Workforce Index (KGWI) seeks the views of respondents in some 30 countries, comprising Gen Y, Gen X and Baby Boomers.

The findings provide a valuable snapshot of just how the different generations in the workforce view some of the key issues that affect work and employment – issues such as training, skills, job mobility, ethics, technology, environmental sustainability, remuneration, globalization, and the role of social media in finding work.

Across each of the surveys, there is a picture emerging of a workforce that is more dynamic, flexible, and one seeking greater engagement with work and wanting to reach new levels of skill. The shape of the labor market is being driven by a more global approach to work; where individuals are willing to move for the right job, and where certain jobs can be performed in many different parts of the world.

There is also a new focus on training and skills development, as the pathway to expertise that will enable individuals to withstand career turbulence and economic uncertainty. Even on a more intangible level, there is evidence about the 'value' of work, that goes beyond the direct financial rewards and touches on the dignity and identity that people derive from their jobs.

The explosion of social networking has opened up a whole new area for individuals to seek out work opportunities and discuss work, but also a platform for people to develop sophisticated online personas and to embark on their own personal marketing or 'branding'

For each generation, there are different priorities. Younger workers in the Gen Y group naturally have longer time horizons and their careers in front of them. They have fewer financial commitments and are generally more willing to assume some element of risk with jobs and careers. Gen X are in the prime of their careers, generally with families and financial commitments. Baby boomers will have a different set of priorities and timescale, developed after a lifetime in the workforce and an entirely different learning experience.

One of the enduring lessons from the academic business literature centers on the value that organizations derive from decision-making that is founded on a diversity of knowledge and opinion. Decisions that flow from a variety of inputs are, on the whole, superior to those that eventuate from just a few sources – what's commonly known as 'group think'.

The source of that diversity may vary. It may be generational, geographic, ethnic, occupational or socio-economic. In coming to complex decisions, it almost always pays to have as many varied inputs as possible. One of the critical advantages in a multi-generational workforce is the incredible diversity it can provide.

For managers, a multi-generational workforce may seem the source of much frustration, though it need not be. The challenge lays in recognizing both the similarities between the generations as well as the areas of divergence, and putting into practice measures that address each group's priorities and interests. Businesses that can manage and capitalize on the generational divide actually have an enormous source of competitive advantage at their fingertips.

The trends and attitudes displayed in the KGWI surveys are revealing, but what should companies do with that information? With four generations in the workplace simultaneously, managers need to understand how to deal with the dynamics of change and how to maximize performance. One of the realities of this new era in workforce planning is that a new generation of employees is moving in and assuming many of the tasks and responsibilities, including many leadership roles, previously held by the baby boomers.

One of the key issues for enterprises is how to provide the emerging generations with the opportunities and challenges they deserve, while retaining the substantial repository of acquired knowledge held by the Baby Boomers. Managing this migration from the mindset of Baby Boomers to the viewpoints of Gen X and Y becomes critical. Figure 9 below encapsulates these different mindsets in four key areas.

FIGURE 9.
Generational mindset differences

	BABY BOOMERS	GENERATIONS X AND Y
Work/Life Balance	'Live to Work'	'Work to Live'
Job Stability	Seek job stability, security	Are comfortable with job changes
Job Expectations	Respect Authority Expect to have and to earn rewards	Question formal authority Want immediate payoffs Demand change and fun
Technology	Learned as adults	Technologically savvy

Recruiting and Training Strategies

One of the most challenging aspects of managing a multi-generational workforce is overcoming the stereotypes inherent in traditional staffing strategies. Companies need to realize that the landscape has changed.

- Hiring managers need to be educated about the war for talent and the contributions offered by free agents. Because many companies are now using a just-in-time workforce and the job market is packed with free agents, job applicant resumes may not show large chunks of time spent with employers. But rather than being concerned by short employment lifecycles, hiring managers should evaluate the knowledge that workers have gained and the skills they have accumulated as a result of working for different employers in various positions.

- The age of the 9 to 5 workday is long gone. Companies must offer employees flexibility in work schedules and supportive structures, allowing people to build their own schedules that fit their work styles and their lifestyles. These changes are most important with Gen Y workers, who are perfectly comfortable making sideways career moves that years ago would have sounded a career death knell. Instead of climbing a corporate ladder, Gen Y workers are focused on a career lattice— lateral movement that brings new opportunities, chances for development, and intellectual challenges. These days a resume peppered with a variety of jobs doesn't indicate an unstable employment history; it means that the candidate has had the chance to learn more skills and become more marketable, and probably more valuable. Gone are the days of a resume showing several decades of working for the same employer.

- Employers need to consider how each generational group interacts with other groups and with management, and focus on building teams—not just across generations, but across cultures as well. Exploiting the different strategies, insights, and ideas provided by multi-generational project teams can help increase productivity, efficiency, and quality.

- Employees should be educated on the benefits and challenges of generational diversity. Understanding the differences in values, work styles, and behaviors helps everyone understand the needs of each group. Taking proactive steps to build knowledge and empathy among all employees will keep different groups from judging others for their perspectives, desires, demands, and expectations.

- Companies need to start building benefits programs to leverage different workforce expectations. Retirement policies may be key to retaining experienced workers who have reached retirement age but want to continue working. Investments in 'reinventing' or 'transitioning' retirees will help keep workers in the labor force longer.

- Offering flexible options and performance rewards can help increase retention of Gen X workers. Training programs geared toward Gen Y workers will help to promote the growth of that segment of the workforce and boost retention rates by keeping employees engaged.

- In today's project-driven business landscape, companies need to streamline staffing strategies by developing hiring practices that enable ease of entry and exit from the organization. Companies can quickly ramp up or scale down their workforce as needed.

Retention Strategies

Well-developed recruiting strategies that make a company attractive as an employer will help entice and recruit top talent. But hiring the right people is only half the battle—retention is equally important.

- To appeal to the widest pool of candidates, companies should build flexible work schedules and the physical and technological infrastructure to support them. Start out by establishing policies about flexible work schedules that will enhance employees' work/life balance without adversely affecting their productivity.

- Invest in technology for mobile offices and online information sharing so flexibility can be seamlessly integrated into the work environment.

- Institute and encourage 'career development' conversations with employees. Keep employees engaged by offering accelerated onboarding programs and cross-functional rotational work programs that offer lateral movement and prevent boredom. Provide opportunities for Gen Y workers to attain career goals that are self-defined, not pre-defined.

- Organize multi-generational project teams that will engage and empower Gen X, Gen Y, and mature workers to tap into the unique contributions of each group.

- Aggressively manage retirement policies and programs that provide special project opportunities for each generational segment of the workforce. Create mentoring and other internal development programs to encourage workers to share knowledge.

According to Dr. Nancy Ahlrichs, author of Manager of Choice, people will come to a company because of the company's reputation, but they will stay—or not stay—because of a manager. Managers should focus on developing skills in talent scouting and building relationships, trust, skills, and a solid organizational brand. In today's highly competitive global workforce, all generations are looking for innovations in the work environment that will attract them and encourage them to stay. Companies should use whatever tools they can find to connect with all candidates and interact with them in a targeted manner.

Branding and Communication

Companies need to stop thinking of their brand only as their external face to the world, and start thinking of it as an employer brand. The brand as a 'business' may be very different from the brand as an 'employer'. Sure, Google® is a great search engine, but they also have a brand as being a great employer. In order to attract top talent, it's necessary to provide an employee value proposition so candidates clearly see the value on offer.

• Strengthen the organization's recruiting and retention messaging to create a solid employer brand that appeals to all generations. Establish supporting policies and procedures that differentiate product/service and employer branding. Develop hiring strategies that attract and keep the most talented people.

• Build transparent internal and external corporate communication programs. The Internet has commoditized information, and as they say, "information is power." Today's technology allows younger generations much easier access to the truth, so employers should give it to them ahead of time to encourage loyalty and increase employee engagement.

• Create programs that entice the Gen Y community, and integrate other generations in the implementation of those programs. Traditional mentoring and reverse mentoring programs are excellent ways to take advantage of having different generations working together.

• Design and use tools that connect with target candidates in their own voice—but you must know what that is! Key messages, tone, and imagery used in employee communications should be appropriate for the generation they are targeted toward. Millennials in particular are interested in knowing why they should come and work for you.

• Consider designating someone to be a Chief Reputation Officer to protect your employer brand. The reputation of your company doesn't depend only on how much people like your products and services—your reputation as an employer can affect your reputation as a company.

SUCCESS STORIES

Companies everywhere are sitting up and taking notice of the shift in control that's taking place in the workforce. With skilled employees in demand and jobs plentiful, some employers have taken bold and unprecedented steps toward making their workplace more enticing so they can attract the best workers and retain them.

Cisco Systems

Cisco, a leader in advanced network technologies, goes to great effort to create a workforce that maximizes collaboration, and engages employees of all generations. The company has aggressively hired Gen Ys who will soon supplant Baby Boomers as the largest generation in the company. There is an almost fanatical preoccupation with communicating to employees the company's 'big picture' vision of strategy and future development. It uses Web 2.0 technologies to increase interactions across its virtual and global workforce.

The company puts a big investment into career development by identifying individual's strengths and allocating roles that capitalize on those strengths. Executives are encouraged to help individuals build a very clear picture of what a future career path will look like. They also recognize that lifestyle and health are important, and that a major area for disengagement is through health problems. The firm's wellness center at its headquarters in San Jose serves 18,000 employees and their dependents.

Its management structure is founded on maximizing collaboration and engagement. A complex network of cross functional councils and boards are the primary source of decision-making. Those who are in this creative loop have a rich source of input from a multi-generational perspective, and are actively engaged, not just in performing work, but contributing to the direction and strategy of the firm.

L'Oreal

L'Oreal, a world leader in the cosmetics industry has won a number of international awards for best practice in managing diversity in the workforce. It places a very high emphasis on diversity in all its forms as part of its culture and its operating principles. Diversity is stressed at every level – the individual, the teams and even among its clients.

The achievement of a diverse organization is facilitated by its structure which promotes autonomy and collaboration, and has a distinct lack of hierarchy, even to the point of emphasizing oral communication over written procedures.

With more than 50,000 employees worldwide, L'Oreal has a dedicated program to encourage career development and employee engagement, built on a system of employee stimulation, training and education, and appraisal. Employees are aided in their career development by a system of promotions to encourage cross-functional learning, with geographic promotion encouraged across the enterprise.

L'Oreal takes an intense interest in the individual, with regular evaluation to determine the needs and professional aspirations of each, so that they have a defined expansion plan within the company.

Sodexo Health Care

Sodexo Health Care needs a very considerable workforce to meets its growth plans. It is expected to hire some two million people over the next decade. To meet that target, it needs managers and staff from all generations. Juggling that workforce to achieve optimum performance is a skill that it has been developing over a number of years.

In essence, the key is in the culture. Sodexo has developed a culture of employee engagement that maximizes service quality while addressing key goals of the individual. It's also about ensuring that Sodexo's external focus is in line with what employees expect, so that there is no mismatch between what they are expected to do and what they feel is appropriate.

The Health care division manages food and facilities for almost 2,000 sites in the United States. Employees are engaged in acute hospital care, aged care and retirement facilities. It's vitally important that employees care about what they do.

Central to their employee engagement strategy is the CARE training program; it emphasizes Compassion, Accountability, Respect, Enthusiasm and Service. They also employ in-field training to improve performance by dealing with various elements of diversity including gender and generational differences. Employees are immersed in highly interactive sessions to help them deal with diversity issues that may arise in the workforce or on the job.

It has embraced technology to help drive the uptake of its training modules and to promote discussion and debate about critical issues. Flexible work options such as shorter working hours for older employees and job sharing have helped to transcend the generational differences and encourage retention.

Another technique has been the adoption of 'storytelling' where people from all generations talk about the way they help change people's lives. It's become a compelling way of imparting the unique culture of the organization and also a tool to build a bridge between different generations of workers.

Best Buy

Global retail giant Best Buy took workforce innovation to a new level with a radical experiment designed to reshape the workplace and redefine the meaning of work itself. At its Minneapolis headquarters, the company's Results-Only Work Environment (ROWE) offers workers an extraordinary degree of work/life balance by doing away with most of the rules and restrictions that have traditionally applied to corporate jobs.

Employees can decide how, when, and where they do their work. They are not expected to keep regular hours or even show up at the office every morning. They can work at the office, in a spare bedroom, on the subway, or in a corner café, and they are required to put in only as much time as they need to get their work done. Hourly employees still must work a certain number of hours in order to comply with federal labor regulations, but they can choose when they want to work those hours.

Supervisors encourage interaction between employees, and workers are not criticized for spending too much time socializing or leaving early to take their child to soccer practice. Attending meetings in person is usually optional. The only criteria managers use to evaluate employees is whether or not they meet established productivity goals.

ROWE has significantly impacted the company in many ways, but the most measurable impact is in the statistics. Productivity at Best Buy headquarters increased by 41 percent, and voluntary turnover in some divisions decreased by up to 90 percent.

The cost of turnover per employee today can be in excess of $100,000, so the reduction in turnover at Best Buy has resulted in a stunning financial payoff for the company. The success of the initial experiment led to the company switching the headquarters campus to ROWE on a division-by-division basis in 2002. So far, 60 percent of the 4,000 people at the headquarters have converted to the new way of working.

Google

Google is another corporate giant famous for shaking up the traditional view of the workplace. The top-ranked search engine also continually takes the top spot in lists of best places to work, because the company regularly invests money in their employees to keep them happy and make sure they love their jobs. Fortune magazine estimated that Google spends $72 million dollars a year just on free food for their employees.

Google campuses worldwide are designed to be fun and pleasant places to work. Offices around the world offer such benefits as massages, laundry machines, gyms, organic food, bike repairs, volleyball courts, swings, table tennis, and on-site doctors. Employees have the best technology available to do their jobs, and the company encourages them to spend 20 percent of their time working on projects that contribute to their personal growth.

With its bold and innovative approach, Google hit on an idea that has been hugely successful. Creating an attractive, enticing work environment keeps people on campus engaged and innovative. Job turnover rates are dramatically low and competition is fierce among job candidates, with Google receiving more than 1,500 applications a day.

CONCLUSION

SURVIVING AND SUCCEEDING

With the global workforce aging and declining, it is the right time for companies to develop strategies for recruiting and retaining top talent from all generations. For workforce planning to be effective, HR managers need to sharpen their skills in interpreting and using workforce data to track trends and assess global insights. Knowing what attracts and keeps employees in their jobs is key to ensuring employee growth and satisfaction while supporting corporate goals and containing costs.

The colliding trends in the workforce are not going to change, and the challenges they present aren't going away. Companies need to act to create a talent management strategy that conquers those challenges. By measuring, developing, and nurturing its human capital, an organization can ensure that its most valuable asset is used effectively and efficiently.

REFERENCES

The Aspen Institute – Domestic Strategy Group. Grow Faster Together, or Grow Slowly Apart. How Will America Work in the 21st Century? 2003

Awases, M., A. Gbary, and R. Chatora. 2003. Migration of Health Professionals in Six Countries: A Synthesis Report. Brazzaville: World Health Organization, Regional Office for Africa.

Chambers, E., Foulon, M., Handfield-Jones, H, Hankin, S., and Michaels, E. 'The War for Talent.' The McKinsey Quarterly, August 1998.

Demographic and Social Trends Issue Paper: 'Europe's Changing Demography Constraints and Bottlenecks,' June 1999

Holleran, Michael J. 'The Talent War: Attracting and Retaining Generation Y Leaders in Professional Services.' Society for Marketing Professional Services, August 2008.

Kelly U.S. Free Agent Survey 2008

Kelly Temporary Analysis Reports

Kiger, Patrick. 'Throwing Out the Rules of Work.' Workforce Management. http://www.workforce.com/section/hr-management/feature/throwing-out-rules-work/index.html

Lam Peng Er, 'Declining Fertility Rates in Japan: An Ageing Crisis Ahead.' EAI Background Brief No. 433. http://www.eai.nus.edu.sg/BB433.pdf

'Living Happily Ever After: The Economic Implications of Aging Societies.' Watson Wyatt Worldwide & World Economic Forum, no date available

Lopatto, Elizabeth. 'Babies Are In: Fertility Rates Increasing in Developed Nations.' Bloomberg Businessweek, August 5, 2009. http://www.bloomberg.com/apps/news?pid=newsarchive&sid=ac7nDxl6G8U4

Madland, David, & Kazzi, Nayla. 'Mixed News for Older Workers.' September 4, 2009. Center for American Progress. http://www.americanprogress.org/issues/2009/09/older_worker.html

'Not a Lost Generation, but a 'Disappointed' One: The Job Market's Impact on Millennials.' The Wharton School of the University of Pennsylvania, Knowledge@Wharton, October 27, 2010. http://knowledge.wharton.upenn.edu/article.cfm?articleid=2619

Richards, Lance Jensen. 'Talent Tsunami: The Seven Waves of Change.' Kelly Outsourcing and Consulting Group.

'Smashing the Clock.' Bloomberg Businessweek, December 11, 2006. (Best Buy's ROWE)http://www.businessweek.com/magazine/content/06_50/b4013001.htm

Staffing Industry Analysts, 2010

Tapscott, Don, & Williams, Anthony. 'Innovating the 21st-Century University: It's Time!' EDUCAUSE Review, Volume 45, Number 1, January/February 2010.

United States Bureau of Labor Statistics: Overview of the 2008-18 Projections

World Population Prospects: The 2006 Revision. United Nations Department of Economic and Social Affairs, Population Division, 2007. http://www.un.org/esa/population/publications/wpp2006/WPP2006_Highlights_rev.pdf

Generational definitions supplied by Wikipedia.org; MRI Data; American Demographics Magazine

www.ingramcontent.com/pod-product-compliance
Lightning Source LLC
Chambersburg PA
CBHW032014190326
41520CB00007B/477